EDGE
BOOKS

OCICATS

by Joanne Mattern

CAPSTONE PRESS
a capstone imprint

Edge Books are published by Capstone Press,
151 Good Counsel Drive, P.O. Box 669, Mankato, Minnesota 56002.
www.capstonepub.com

 Books published by Capstone Press are manufactured with paper
containing at least 10 percent post-consumer waste.

Library of Congress Cataloging-in-Publication Data
Mattern, Joanne, 1963–
    Ocicats / by Joanne Mattern.
        p. cm.—(Edge books. All about cats)
    Includes bibliographical references and index.
    Summary: "Describes the history, physical features, temperament, and care of the
Ocicat cat breed"—Provided by publisher.
    ISBN 978-1-4296-6633-6 (library binding)
    1. Ocicat—Juvenile literature. I. Title.
    SF449.O35M382 2011
    636.8'2—dc22   2010039956

Editorial Credits
Connie R. Colwell and Carrie Braulick Sheely, editors; Heidi Thompson, designer;
    Wanda Winch, media researcher; Eric Manske, production specialist

Photo Credits
Alamy: Tierfotoagentur, cover; Newscom: Sipa Press/Shiho Fukada, 12; Photo
by Fiona Green, 6, 9 (inset), 11, 19, 21, 23, 25, 26, 28; Rom Kimball Stock: Ron
Kimball Studios, 5, 10, 15, 17; Shutterstock: Glen Gaffney, 9

Printed in the United States of America in Stevens Point, Wisconsin.
092010   005934WZS11

TABLE OF CONTENTS

Chapter 1

A WALK ON THE WILD SIDE

When seeing an Ocicat for the first time, some people wonder if it is tame or wild. The Ocicat's spotted coat makes it look like a wildcat. But the Ocicat does not have a wild personality. It is a friendly cat that is as tame as members of other domestic cat breeds.

In 2009 the Ocicat was the 20th most popular breed in the Cat Fanciers' Association (CFA). The CFA is the largest cat registry in the world. It recognizes and tracks ancestries for more than 40 breeds.

Much of the Ocicat's popularity has to do with its appearance. The Ocicat is the only spotted domestic breed developed specifically to look like a wildcat. Ocicats also have agouti coats, which adds to their unique look.

domestic—no longer wild; people keep domestic animals as pets

agouti—a coat that has bands of light and dark color on each hair; an agouti coat is sometimes called a ticked coat

FACT: Most cats dislike water. But many Ocicats seem to enjoy playing in it.

The Ocicat's unique spotted coat pattern attracts many people to the breed.

FACT: Ocicats are a vocal breed, but they don't have the raspy yowl of their Siamese relatives.

An Ocicat that has another cat to play with is less likely to become bored when its owners are away.

IS AN OCICAT RIGHT FOR YOU?

Ocicats make great family pets for many households. Ocicats are healthy and need little special care. These friendly, curious cats seem to like being around people.

Ocicats are very social. They enjoy the company of both cats and dogs. If you're away from home often, it's best to have a companion animal for your Ocicat.

You can find an Ocicat in several ways. Many people buy Ocicats from breeders. Breeders often charge several hundred dollars for an Ocicat. Other people adopt Ocicats from rescue organizations. These groups help find new homes for cats of a certain breed. Cats adopted from rescue organizations usually are less expensive than those sold by breeders. Some cats may even be registered.

Occasionally, people can adopt Ocicats from animal shelters. But most shelters have mixed-breed cats instead of purebred cats such as the Ocicat.

Chapter 2

OCICAT HISTORY

Compared to other cat breeds, the Ocicat is fairly new. The first Ocicats were bred about 50 years ago. Ocicats are mostly Siamese, but they also are part Abyssinian.

TONGA

In 1964 a Michigan cat breeder named Virginia Daly was working toward a goal. She was trying to produce a Siamese cat with colorpoints that looked like an Abyssinian's agouti coat.

Daly first bred an Abyssinian and a Siamese cat. She named a female kitten from this mating Dalai She. Daly then bred Dalai She to a Siamese named Whitehead Elegante Sun. When Daly mated these two cats again, she got a surprise. One kitten from this mating didn't look like the other cats the matings had produced. This kitten had ivory fur and bright golden spots. Daly named the cat Tonga. Daly's daughter called him an "ocicat" because Tonga looked like a wildcat called the ocelot. Daly had Tonga neutered so he could not reproduce. She then sold him as a pet.

colorpoint—a pattern in which the ears, face, tail, and feet are darker than the base color

The ocelot and the Ocicat (inset) have similar spotted patterns.

A NEW BREED TAKES OFF

Daly later wrote to Dr. Clyde Keeler of Georgia University. Keeler was interested in creating a cat that looked like the Egyptian Spotted Fishing Cat. This extinct cat lived in ancient Egypt.

Daly told Keeler that she had produced a spotted cat. Keeler encouraged Daly to try to make a new cat breed by producing more spotted kittens.

Daly bred Tonga's parents again. They produced what Daly had hoped for—another spotted kitten. Daly named this kitten Dalai Dotson. Dalai Dotson and other spotted kittens like him soon became known as Ocicats.

Other breeders began working with Ocicats. They bred some Ocicats with American Shorthairs. Breeding with American Shorthairs gave Ocicats larger, stronger bodies.

The American Shorthair is one of the oldest native cat breeds in the United States.

In 2004 Ocicat Moirai Wedjat won the "Best of the Best" prize at a CFA show at Madison Square Garden in New York.

Ocicats began appearing at cat shows in the late 1960s. The International Cat Association (TICA) officially recognized the breed in 1986. In 1987 the CFA recognized the Ocicat.

GAINING POPULARITY

After the CFA recognized the Ocicat, the breed quickly gained popularity. By 1988 the Ocicat was the 14th most popular breed out of 35 CFA breeds.

The Ocicat also quickly earned awards at CFA shows. In September 1987, an Ocicat was named a Grand Champion for the first time. In the 1991–1992 show season, an Ocicat received a National Winner title for the first time. Since then, Ocicats have won many important CFA titles and awards.

 **FACT:** In the early 1990s, Ocicats were separated into color classes for CFA shows. Before this time, Ocicats of all colors competed in the same class.

Chapter 3

STRONG AND SPOTTED

Ocicats are medium to large in size. Males usually weigh 11 to 14 pounds (5 to 6.4 kilograms). Females are smaller. They usually weigh between 6 and 10 pounds (2.7 and 4.5 kg).

BODY

The Ocicat's body is solid and muscular. Long, strong legs help support its frame. The shoulders and chest are deep and broad. The back is level or slightly higher in the rear.

Although the Ocicat is strong, it isn't bulky. Instead, the Ocicat has the sleek, graceful appearance of a well-trained athlete. The cat's dense bones and muscles make it feel heavier than it looks.

An Ocicat's short, smooth fur lies close to its body. The coat is glossy and feels soft like satin.

Ocicats have well-developed muscles.

PATTERNS AND COLORS

The Ocicat's agouti coat has a dark spotted pattern on a lighter background color. Background coat colors come in tawny, ivory, honey, blue, and silver. Tawny is a ticked brown color. Blue is a blue-gray color, and silver is almost white.

An Ocicat's thumb-shaped spots can be black, chocolate, cinnamon, fawn, blue, or lavender. Fawn is a light shade of the red-brown cinnamon color. Lavender is a lighter shade of chocolate that has a pink tint. An Ocicat's spots always are darker than the rest of the fur. At cat shows, judges prefer well-defined spots instead of faint ones.

 **FACT:** Sometimes breeders have difficulty deciding the color of an Ocicat. In these cases, they use the tail tip to identify the correct color.

Ocicats can have one of several background colors, including silver (left) and tawny (right).

The CFA accepts Ocicats in 12 color patterns. These patterns come from combinations of background and spot colors. Six of the colors are based off the silver background. They are ebony silver, chocolate silver, cinnamon silver, blue silver, lavender silver, and fawn silver.

The other six color patterns have varying backgrounds according to the spot color. These patterns are tawny, chocolate, cinnamon, blue, lavender, and fawn.

Some Ocicats do not meet the breed standard. These cats may be solid colored or have tabby stripes rather than spots. Ocicats without spots cannot compete in CFA cat shows.

FACIAL FEATURES

Like the Siamese cat, the Ocicat has a wedge-shaped head. Its ears are alert and wide. The ears may have pointed tufts of hair at the tips. The Ocicat's large, almond-shaped eyes angle toward the ears.

breed standard—certain physical features in a breed that judges look for in a cat show

Ocicats have an M-shaped marking on their foreheads.

 FACT: The lightest color on an Ocicat's coat is usually found on the chin, lower jaw, and around the eyes.

PERSONALITY

Many people say the Ocicat's personality is more like a dog than a cat. Ocicats seem to enjoy spending time with their owners. The cats often follow their owners from room to room. Some Ocicats will ride on their owners' shoulders.

Ocicats are smart. They sometimes can be trained to do tricks and walk on a leash. Some owners teach their Ocicats to fetch.

Ocicats are an active breed. But they are less active than some of their shorthaired cousins such as the Oriental. The Ocicat's athletic build helps it jump high and run quickly.

 **FACT:** Many owners bring their Ocicats along when they travel. The cats easily adjust to new surroundings.

Leaving toys out for your Ocicat will help keep it active while you are away.

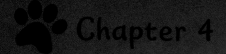

Chapter 4

CARING FOR AN OCICAT

The Ocicat is a strong, healthy breed. With good care, Ocicats can live 15 to 20 years.

You can help your cat live a longer, healthier life by keeping it inside. Some cat owners let their cats roam outdoors. Cats that roam outdoors often catch serious diseases from other animals. Outdoor cats may also be injured by cars or other animals.

FEEDING

Like all cats, Ocicats need a balanced, nutritious diet. Both dry and moist food are suitable for Ocicats. Dry food usually is less expensive than moist food. Eating dry food helps clean a cat's teeth. Dry food will not spoil if it is left in a dish, but moist food can spoil easily. Moist food should not be left out for more than one hour.

Some owners fill their cats' dishes with dry food and allow their cats to eat throughout the day.

23

The amount of food needed depends on your cat's size and appetite. You can use the feeding instructions on the pet food package as a guide. A veterinarian can also help you decide how much to feed your cat.

Owners should make sure their cats' water bowls are always filled. Cats need to drink plenty of water to stay healthy. You should change the water each day to keep it clean.

LITTER BOXES

Your Ocicat will need a litter box where it can get rid of bodily waste. There are several types of litter to choose from. Clay litter is the most popular. Litter made of pine wood, corn, and recycled newspaper is also available. Your cat may prefer one type over another.

Be sure to clean the waste out of the box each day. Change the litter about every two weeks. Cats are clean animals and may refuse to use a dirty litter box.

litter—small bits of clay or other material used to absorb the waste of cats and other animals

SCRATCHING POSTS

Cats mark their territories by scratching objects to leave their scent. Cats also scratch to release tension and to sharpen their claws. When cats scratch indoors, they can damage furniture, carpets, or curtains. To prevent damage, owners should provide their cats with a scratching post. You can buy a scratching post at pet stores. You can also make one by attaching carpet to a small wooden post.

Many scratching posts are made with a strong rope called sisal.

Weekly brushing will help keep
your Ocicat's coat healthy and shiny.

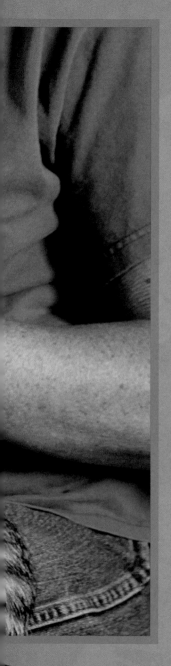

GROOMING

An Ocicat's short coat needs little grooming. Ocicats should be brushed with a soft bristle or rubber brush weekly.

After brushing, you should use a coarse comb to smooth out your cat's fur. Some owners rub their Ocicats with a soft cloth called a chamois. The chamois helps keep an Ocicat's coat shiny.

Regular brushing helps prevent hairballs. Large hairballs can block the digestive system. A vet may have to remove these hairballs.

NAIL CARE

Ocicats need their nails trimmed every few weeks. This practice reduces damage if cats scratch household furniture. Nail trimmers made for cats are available at pet stores. These trimmers are easy to handle and reduce the risk of injury to your cat.

A cat can get ingrown nails if its nails are not trimmed regularly. A cat with ingrown nails has claws that have grown into the pad or bottom of the paw. This growth can cause serious and painful infections.

Owners should begin trimming a cat's nails when it is a kitten. The kitten will become used to having its nails trimmed as it grows older.

hairball—a ball of fur that lodges in a cat's stomach; hairballs are made of fur swallowed by the cat as it grooms itself

DENTAL CARE

All cats need regular dental care to protect their teeth and gums from plaque. Brush your cat's teeth at least once a week. Use a cloth or a special toothbrush made for cats. Never brush your cat's teeth with toothpaste made for people. It can make your cat sick. Instead, buy a toothpaste made for cats from a pet store.

As cats grow older, they may have more plaque and other dental problems. Owners should then have a veterinarian clean a cat's teeth.

Brushing your cat's teeth weekly will help prevent gum disease and tooth decay.

plaque—the coating of food, saliva, and bacteria that forms on teeth and can cause tooth decay

HEALTH CARE

Ocicats need regular checkups by a veterinarian. Most vets recommend yearly visits for cats. Older cats may need vet visits two or three times each year.

People who buy an Ocicat should take it to a vet as soon as possible. There are no specific health problems linked to the Ocicat breed. But the vet will check your cat for any signs of health problems. The vet will also give your cat any necessary vaccinations.

Veterinarians also spay and neuter cats. These surgeries make it impossible for cats to reproduce. Owners who do not plan to breed their cats should have them spayed or neutered. The surgeries keep unwanted kittens from being born. They also can help keep your cat from developing certain diseases.

The wild look and fun personality of Ocicats make them unique treasures of the cat world. Taking good care of your Ocicat can bring many years of companionship with your feline friend.

vaccination—a shot of medicine that protects animals from a disease

GLOSSARY

agouti (uh-GOO-tee)—a coat that has bands of light and dark color on each hair; an agouti coat is sometimes called a ticked coat

breed (BREED)—a certain kind of animal within an animal group; breed also means to mate and raise a certain kind of animal

breed standard (BREED STAN-durd)—certain physical features in a breed that judges look for at a cat show

colorpoint (KUHL-ur-point)—a pattern in which the ears face, tail, and feet are darker than the base color

domestic (duh-MES-tik)—no longer wild; people keep domestic animals as pets

hairball (HAIR-bawl)—a ball of fur that lodges in a cat's stomach; hairballs are made of fur swallowed by a cat as it grooms itself

litter (LIT-ur)—small bits of clay or other material used to absorb the waste of cats and other animals

plaque (PLAK)—the coating of food, saliva, and bacteria that forms on teeth and can cause tooth decay

registry (REH-juh-stree)—an organization that keeps track of the ancestry for cats of a certain breed

vaccination (vak-suh-NAY-shun)—a shot of medicine that protects animals from a disease

READ MORE

Britton, Tamara L. *Abyssinian Cats.* Cats. Edina, Minn.: ABDO Publishing Company, 2011.

Mattern, Joanne. *American Shorthair Cats.* All About Cats. Mankato, Minn.: Capstone Press, 2011.

Rau, Dana Meachen. *Top 10 Cats for Kids.* Top Pets for Kids With American Humane. Berkeley Heights, N.J.: Enslow Elementary, 2009.

INTERNET SITES

FactHound offers a safe, fun way to find Internet sites related to this book. All of the sites on FactHound have been researched by our staff.

Here's all you do:

Visit *www.facthound.com*

Type in this code: 9781429666336

Check out projects, games and lots more at
www.capstonekids.com

INDEX